D0282786

GRACENOMICS

UNLEASH THE POWER OF SECOND CHANCE LIVING

©2010 People of the Second Chance
PO Box 77862
Corona, CA 92877
www.POTSC.com
CONTACT@POTSC.com

Cover design and book layout by PlainJoe Studios. www.plainjoe.net
Author photograph by Trevor Hoehne.

In certain cases, the names have been changed in order to protect the privacy of the
individuals mentioned in this book.

Also available as an audio book or e-book.

Printed in the United States of America

Visit www.POTSC.com

10 9 8 7 6 5 4 3 2 1

FOR MY BRIDE, PRINCE AND PRINCESS.

YOU ARE THE BEST PART OF MY LIFE.

TABLE OF CONTENTS

GRACE MATTERS

POUNDING BEATS OF GRACE

In 1998, a band on the stage of a tiny club in Tel Aviv made history.

But it wasn't the kind of history the world had come to expect from headlines about this region.

It wasn't another casualty in the ongoing Israeli-Palestinian conflict that claimed 38 lives in 1998. Nor was it another peace agreement like the Wye River Memorandum signed in October that year.

It was much simpler than that.

Six unlikely members of a band took their spots to play for a small town club audience. The only thing separating this particular gig from thousands of others across the world was one minor detail: the band's members were drawn from two people groups who happened to be at war with each other.

Mark, from Israel, was on bass.

Shadi, from the Gaza Strip in Palestine, played the keyboard.

Yassin and Gani were on vocals and Zaher and Katia filled in with strings and percussion. All in all, three band members were from Israel and three were from Palestine.

They called themselves White Flag and their performance was just that - a tiny symbol of grace in the middle of the historic, explosive conflict between Palestine and Israel.

For one night, acceptance and understanding replaced violence and hate on the set list.

And, in that moment, White Flag taught the world a simple and transformative truth.

Grace is possible.

But before we go much further let me introduce myself.

My name is Mike.

I live in California, but I hate sand. And no, I don't surf. I hate the water too.

I consider myself a certified member of the Apple cult. My latest crush is on the MacBook Pro.

When I tell people what music I listen to, I usually get the same reaction: "WHO??" But I just don't understand how people could not know or be deeply affected by the musical styling of *The Antlers* and *The Books* or *Freelance Whales*. (See? I warned you.)

But don't worry. You've at least heard of the stuff in my magazine rack: Fast Company, Esquire, WIRED... oh, and People Magazine. (It's my guilty obsession.)

To sum it all up, I'm just a regular guy you could grab a beer with. Especially if, on a special occasion, you're up for a chilled bottle of Dos Esquis before lunch. It is my definition of a champagne brunch. Stay thirsty, my friend.

GRACENOMICS = BUILDING AND SUSTAINING AN ECONOMY OF GRACE.

At nine years old, I launched my first venture as a makeshift street vendor, pawning off avocados from my parents' tree. At twelve, I had a thriving lawn mowing business that happily serviced my entire neighborhood's fescue needs. Years later I added a rock band and a pool cleaning business to my résumé.

Then, in 2001 my friend and I started PlainJoe Studios, a design firm in Southern California where I still serve on the Executive Team. Thanks to the most talented team of creative minds in the country, PlainJoe has become an award winning national firm.

Though selling avocados and working at PlainJoe has been rewarding work, my real passion is broken people. Over the past decade I've dedicated myself to helping people who've been branded as failures unleash a second chance life.

During this time, I have personally researched and studied the human condition. I have traveled tens-of-thousands of miles learning and speaking about failure, including moving my family to Asia for a season.

I have enjoyed this direction so much that what started out as an interest has become THE driving passion of my life. I have dedicated the rest of my life to helping leaders manage personal crisis and build sustainable lives.

All this led to starting *People of the Second Chance*, an organization I founded with my best friend Jud Wilhite.

So, what is *People of the Second Chance*? I'm glad you asked.

People of the Second Chance is a movement of people committed to showing unexpected, excessive and scandalous amounts of grace.

Together we're setting out to be the first in line to forgive.
We're racing to release grudges.
We're making room for those on life's margins.
We're raising our voices for the vulnerable.
We're accepting the unacceptable.

We're becoming the Red Cross relief team for the disasters in people's personal lives.

We're setting out to be the living, breathing PEZ dispensers of grace for our world.

Click our heads back and out pops forgiveness for our enemies. Pop us again and you get healing words for the wounded. Click us once more to score friendship through devastating pain. Pop it back again and again and again and the response will always be a sweet delectable second chance. We are grace dispensers who practice second chance living.

PERSON OF NO REPUTATION

One more thing you need to know about me: over time, I've come to consider myself to be a **person of no reputation.** Here's why: I've discovered when you give up your reputation, you don't have to spend so much time and energy defending it.

Unfortunately, I figured this out the hard way.

For most of my adult life, I used my design skills to create cover-ups to hide my failures and dysfunctions.

The problem with this plan, of course, was that maintaining a publicly acceptable version of Mike Foster became my full time job on top of my actual full time job. Over time, this became one too many full time jobs.

In hiding my weaknesses, I eventually realized I had been denying something really important: the real me.

And as much as I hate to admit it, the less desirable parts of myself are still me.

In fact, those traits are just as much me as any of my strengths or accomplishments.

Trying to cut free of my flaws, then, was no more logical than trying to saw off a broken arm. Sure, a broken limb isn't necessarily pretty or fully functional but, with some healing, it still holds potential to contribute. Good or bad, it's still connected to the whole; it's still a part of the story.

That got me on the road I'm on now, hanging out with the wrong people, slopping around in messes and pouring my life into what some consider unpopular enterprises.

But I'm not complaining about that. Why would I? I've been freed to be a person of no reputation and you can be too.

WHAT IS GRACENOMICS?

What you have in your hands is different than most books. GRACENOMICS is an appetizer of sorts. It's the start of a larger conversation to come about grace, failure and second chances.

The book is designed for us non-readers—the ADD Twitter junkies that demand easily downloadable information. If I could have said everything in 140 characters, trust me, you would be reading the world's shortest book. I've kept it short and to the point because I'm hoping this is just the orientation to a movement we'll all be part of for years to come.

So, what is GRACENOMICS?

Granted, there are different definitions of grace floating around. But, for our purposes, grace is the act of giving favor when it is not required.

GRACENOMICS, then, combines this definition of grace with the term economics. Just as economics is the science that deals with the production, distribution and consumption of goods and services, GRACENOMICS is the science that deals with the production, distribution and consumption of grace.

As you can probably guess, GRACENOMICS has cultural, religious, political and international implications. But in this little book we'll focus on just a few ways grace expresses itself in:

1. YOU
2. OTHERS
3. THE WORKPLACE

GRACENOMICS
[gray-se-nomics]

-noun

1. The science that deals with the production, distribution and consumption of grace.

JUST THE FACTS JACK

The other day my friend Jeff, who happens to be a Pulitzer Prize winner, sent me an email. Since one of my hard and fast rules in life is to open all emails from Pulitzer Prize winners, I got right on it. Plus, Jeff has never been guilty of forwarding me Lady Gaga gossip or spamming me with URGENT emails declaring Barack Obama is a Socialist.

Inside was a smartly written article assessing whether Millenials were the next "great" generation by Erik Hayden.

The article reported some telling findings from a University of Michigan study which analyzed 72 samples of academic research and surveys from over 14,000 18 to 25-year-old college students.

Their conclusion? Not exactly flattering for the 79 million Millenials who are usually depicted as humanitarians that champion social justice, recycling and saving baby kittens.

Specifically, the research claimed empathy—which, I might suggest, is directly connected to grace—has been declining FOR NEARLY THIRTY YEARS!

And we're not just talking a small, barely noticeable loss of grace. We're talking a 48 percent drop in empathetic concern and a 34 percent decrease in the ability to see others' perspectives. Young people, they concluded, are losing their ability for deep emotional understanding of another's feelings or problems. Surprised at all? I was.

Whether you are a Millenial or not, you might be saying, "Hey, I'm not a judgmental person. I'm open-minded. I cut people slack all the time! I care about people's feelings!" But the results of the study suggest that our grace distribution techniques leave a lot to be desired.

AUTHENTIC HARSHNESS

So, maybe one of the first jobs of GRACENOMICS is raising grace-awareness.

And right now, in the face of unemployment highs and large-scale tragedies, it is the perfect time to tune into the grace shortage in society.

Consider a recent news story that captured the dilemma of Arnold Abbott and Catherine Sims. In 1991, Mr. Abbott started a charity called *Love Thy Neighbor* in memory of his late wife. The charity helps the homeless of Broward County, Florida.

Ms. Sims, on the other hand, owns a jewelry company in Detroit called *Love Your Neighbor*. But more importantly, she legally trademarked the phrase, "love thy neighbor."

So, guess what?

Ms. Sims sued Mr. Abbott claiming that his homeless charity was creating confusion and violating her trademark.

She sued him for damages and told him to stop using the name *Love Thy Neighbor*. Wow!

This is just one example of the epidemic harshness that has crept into our handling of each other. It's not just extreme legal cases like this that demonstrate society's lack of grace, however.

Sometimes grace is drained out of our world by everyday conversation.

Sometimes I worry, for example, that in our rush to champion "authenticity," our generation has mistaken transparency for character.

We aspire to be brutal truth tellers like the shock jocks who entertain us. The more in-your-face, reality-TV-esque, the better.

High school kids nonchalantly forward private pictures of the high school beauty queen with her top off. Office workers post pictures of themselves smashed from their weekend partying. South Carolina Representative Joe Wilson becomes a folk hero after spontaneously shouting, "You lie!" during President Obama's State of the Union address. Even after all the drama our honesty ignites, we keep insisting that unrestrained transparency is respectable.

Case in point? Brad Blanton, a psychotherapist and the founder of the Radical Honesty movement, claims we should seek to remove the filters between our brains and our mouths.

If you think it, just say it. There is no such thing as over-sharing.

Got the hots for your brother's wife? Announce it. Think a co-worker's new cologne smells like a wet horse? Spread the word.

Hiding Anne Frank in your basement? Let the inquiring Nazis know. Just keeping it real, right?

Sound insane? The 175,000 copies of Blanton's books printed in 11 languages seem to suggest he is not alone in his perspective.

It suddenly seems even smarter to buckle down and get a quick education in GRACENOMICS, don't you think?

VULTURE CULTURE

You could say our fixation with harshness has created a "Vulture Culture."

Meaning our world likes to go after the badly injured. We swoop down and pick the meat off of carcasses weakened by scandal, addiction and failure.

Classic example? The headlines that make objective, newsworthy statements like *Elizabeth Lambert: Dirtiest Player in Women's Soccer*. You may remember the story. Lambert, a 20-year-old blonde who played soccer for New Mexico University, was caught by ESPN's cameras grabbing the ponytail of a Brigham Young University opponent and brutally yanking the girl to the ground. Later, she kicked one girl across the chest and another one in the head.

Clearly Lambert was out of line, warranting a suspension from her university. But that consequence wasn't enough for the Vulture Culture.

We were still hungry for human flesh.

And so, online commenters labeled Lambert "a stupid whore" or voiced a desire to "pull [Lambert] down by her hair and cleat her right in her nasty little face." One vulture said watching Lambert's excessively aggressive game play made him "horny" and another wished he could "kick her in her private parts and paralyze her."

It wasn't just a few perverted people feasting on Lambert while she was down though. Over 2.5 million people on YouTube tuned in to watch or re-watch Lambert's actions. And 9,600 plus people left comments, many of which cannot be repeated in this book.

Does anyone else think a little grace could go a long way in this situation?

But it's not really about Lambert, is it?

It's about society's tendency to feast on humiliation. We build people up only to tear them down. It has become a spectator sport of its own.

The Vulture Culture feasts on our humanity and prevents us from seeing each other as equal members of the human race.

For a few minutes of escape, I sometimes visit the website FaceInHole.com, which lets you create a totally "new look" for yourself.

How? By dropping a photo of your face into other photographs on the site.

You can see what you'd look like with Arnold Schwarzenegger's buffed up biceps or Pamela Anderson's bikini assets.

In the spirit of FaceInHole.com, maybe we could try this social experiment.

Next time we're seduced to join the public smack down of someone, let's imagine our faces and families attached to those headlines.

Next time we are invited to feast on the latest victim of the Vulture Culture, let's imagine what it would be like if we were the ones being skewered and barbecued.

With our face in those holes, the judgment slows up considerably, don't you think?

PREYING UPON
PEOPLE WHO
HAVE FAILED
IS SORT OF LIKE
PICKING THE
MEAT OFF
BUFFALO WINGS.

IT'S NEVER PRETTY
FOR OTHER PEOPLE
TO WATCH.

GRACE STALKS

Honestly there are weeks when I think a grace revolution is impossible.

These days it seems as if a second chance is as odd as a two-dollar bill. You know they're out there, but you rarely come across one.

Even as I look at my own history I realize how much I desperately need grace. GRACENOMICS is basically the story of my life.

Every decade of my journey has been stained by a massive personal, professional or relational failure or crisis.

In high school I flourished into a…nerd. Headgear and braces. Acne. Four eyes. Broken front teeth. I was the total package. Occasionally, if I got lucky, I scored hot dates with girls…but only in my mind. There were none in real life however.

My first year in college, I scored straight D's and F's. After four more tortured years of accomplishing nothing academically, I quit.

But school and low self-esteem was only one part of my disastrous start.

Let's talk about work.

In my early twenties I was fired from my job…one week before Christmas…when I was still newly married…just after my first child was born. Did I mention I had no savings?

In 2006 a business I started tanked and ruined my family financially. It was the first time I ever cried in my office.

I created a national advertising campaign condemned by the Little People of America for lighthearted humor about those short in stature. It ended with me making a very big public apology.

Did I mention that along the way, I acquired a criminal record and my very own parole officer for almost accidentally killing a man?

Or that I wrote a leadership book about integrity with my best friend that the publisher pulled after eight weeks due to what some considered to be insensitive material?

This is my history; the rotting breadcrumbs that remind me where I've been. Some of them are still hard to talk about.

But, even in the darkest stretches, I could always hear grace stealthily moving in the background. Lurking in the shadows. I knew it was there. Following close behind.

Perhaps you should consider this a warning, in fact, that by the time you finish this book, the idea of grace may be stalking you too.

A second chance life is waiting for you.

YOUR SCARS

So now it's your turn.

There's no one around right now.

And even if someone is in the room, you're safely lost in a book. They don't know what you're reading.

What you're thinking about.

They don't know if you too have life moments that are still too hard to talk about.

They can't see your scars.

So go ahead. You don't have to be afraid. Let your mind brush over the parts of your story you wish never happened.

The message of GRACENOMICS is for you. I know this because the message of GRACENOMICS is for everyone:

Busted up businessmen starting to drink to forget.

Geeks in marching band just wanting to be noticed.

Social entrepreneurs whose dreams of changing the world aren't changing anyone.

90210 girls who are starving and sucking their bodies into catwalk proportions.

Religious leaders who are gaining the world but losing their souls.

And for the annoying coffee-breath guy, sharing a cubicle with you at the office.

Everyone is a potential customer. And once the virus of a second chance has infected you, you won't be able to stop the grace from spreading.

I don't know about you, but all the headlines, the research, the preying on the weak just confirm what I feel in my gut every time I crack down hard on someone who needs grace.

It just doesn't feel right, does it?

Maybe that's because it *isn't*.

Maybe this wasn't how life was meant to be. Maybe there's a FAR BETTER way.

These "maybes" are exactly what lead me to the underlying premise of this book, that grace can make the world a better place.

Though the obstacles and challenges are significant, I believe now is the time to unleash the power of second chance living.

It is in this unique moment of history that we realize that not only is grace possible, but that grace really does matter.

NOTES. YOUR THOUGHTS. PERSONAL APPLICATION.

GRACENOMICS FOR YOU

STOP INVESTING IN THE (NOT) STOCK

DON'T MAKE A CAREER OUT OF BEING A VICTIM

FIND THE AWESOME

MAKE FRIENDS WITH YOUR SHADOW

TAKE THE LONG VIEW

INSANE IN THE MEMBRANE

Our bodies, as it turns out, have 100 million sensory receptors that allow us to experience the external world we call "reality." These receptors make it possible for human beings to see, hear, taste, touch and smell our physical world.

With 100 million receptors, our bodies are intensely processing our world. However, our bodies are nowhere near as powerfully engaged as our minds.

Our brains have 10,000 billion synapses—100,000 times the bodies' receptors—working constantly to process and tweak everything we know to create an interior reality.

Our interior reality is just ours, of course. No one else lives there.

So it often contains overblown or misplaced amounts of pain, anxiety or depression that no one else examines closely enough to challenge. It seems like our heads are barely inhabitable.

True, our brains may not overtly, purposefully sabotage our own lives. But too often those 10,000 billion firing synapses create real messages that can really jack with us.

Take that ugly, hyper-critical voice that we—for some reason—let operate the PA system in our heads, for example.

You know. That voice that follows our every move. That calls us out on those five extra pounds or that crooked front tooth. That always brings up that night we drank too much or dropped our pants too fast.

Most of us wouldn't choose to hang out with other people who live to criticize us. Yet we let our own self-talk drain the grace out of our lives every single day and we never do a thing about it.

In an era where economic cutbacks are the norm, there's no better time to lay this sucker off and take back control of our mind's PA.

THE (NOT) STOCK

When it comes to self-deprecation, we adopt logic that wouldn't fly anywhere else in our lives.

Take the stock market, for example.

Many of us pride ourselves on being savvy, informed investors. We check out a company's profit history, we read about their CEO's qualifications, we watch the market carefully for signs of change.

We invest only in the best, most promising stocks that will deliver the best return to our wallets.

In a sad, counter-intuitive move, we invest emotionally and psychologically in the messages that are least promising - the stocks that will cost us the most.

Let's call it the (NOT) stock.

You know what I mean.

We're (NOT) thin enough.
We're (NOT) loved by those we want love from.
We're (NOT) making any impact at our job.
We're (NOT) going to kick this addiction.
We're (NOT) going to be able to fix that embarrassing mistake.
We're (NOT) cutting it at school or work.
We're (NOT) going to make it.

And even though we never see any positive dividends, we just keep buying into the stock. We keep investing in messages that lower the value of our life portfolio.

I know about this because I invest in the wrong stocks all the time.

Case in point: I have the privilege of being called Dad by two wonderful children—my eleven year old son, Jackson, and my eight year old daughter, Taylor. It honors me that children like them see fit to call me "Dad." It's hands down the best job description of my life.

But even though parenting is a dominantly positive experience, my brain and its misleading 10 billion synapses constantly sidetracks the goodness I feel by introducing cutting self-talk.

Here's its favorite one-liner: Mike, you're a bad dad.

The thought is disruptive, it plays on my insecurity, it packs guilt on to my daily schedule. It contributes nothing but bad feelings to my life. But you know what is truly tragic? I keep investing in it.

It is one of my go-to (NOT) stocks.

GRACENOMICS TARGET

FAILURES

TARGET MARKET

UNFORGIVENESS

LIVING IN VICTIMVILLE

I take careful notes, reminding myself of my deficits—

The times I failed to play catch in the backyard with Jackson even though I promised I would.

That Saturday morning I lost my temper and caused my daughter to hide in the bathroom for an hour.

I'm reminded of our family vacation in Palm Springs this summer and how I hunkered down in the hotel room writing GRACENOMICS. While other fathers at the resort had a blast with their children in the hotel pool, my kids sadly swam alone. Their dad selfishly chose his little writing career over them.

Though my wife and close friends would probably challenge some of my negative assessments, it doesn't prevent me from investing in this (NOT) stock over and over again.

So when I talk about GRACENOMICS FOR YOU, I just want to be clear. I'm talking about myself too.

So what do we do when we realize there is a shortage of grace in both our exterior and interior worlds?

OPTION #1: WE SCRAPE BY WITHOUT IT.
We gut it out, which leaves us resentful and empty.

OPTION #2: WE PAY MORE FOR GRACE THAN WE WANT TO.
We try to earn acceptance, for example, by becoming a people pleaser.

OPTION #3: WE FIND A SUBSTITUTE FOR GRACE.
This may play out in addictions or other harmful behaviors.

We quiet the voices by introducing them to our new best friends Jack Daniels or Mary Jane.

Or, a better choice: decide that grace—although scarce—is too valuable to live without and choose to make acquiring it our most urgent priority.

Consider the words of Nelson Mandela. "We ask ourselves, 'Who am I to be brilliant, gorgeous, talented, fabulous?' Actually, who are you not to be?"

So let us look at a few strategies that can help unleash GRACENOMICS FOR YOU.

CHEWING ON YOURSELF

Have you ever heard of self-cannibalism?

It's exactly what it sounds like—the practice of eating one's own flesh.

Some people do the fingernail-biting thing. Others like to chew on their own hair. The really extreme dudes bite their skin or drink their own blood.

Ready to puke yet? But here's the thing.

PERSONAL GROWTH

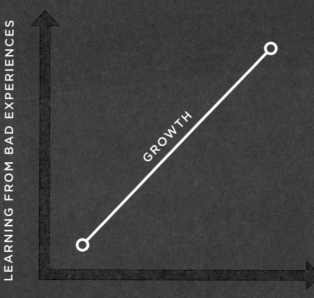

When we adopt a victim persona, I think we hit that same level of gross. We cannibalize ourselves. We feast on our own weaknesses or hardships. We devour our own failure and snack on personal defeatism.

This brings us to the first principle of GRACENOMICS FOR YOU:

DON'T MAKE A CAREER OUT OF BEING A VICTIM.

GRACENOMICS has its own "No Shirt. No Shoes. No Service." Policy. It is simply this: No victims allowed.

Too often we are like Herbie Sperlings. When Herbie was questioned by police about two pistols and an axe used in three murders found in the trunk of his rented car, he replied, "Damned if I know. And you can be f@#kin' sure I'll never rent no car from Avis again."

It's easy to pull a "Herbie" and blame others for your problems. But just as this axe murderer couldn't face his own issues when declaring himself a victim, neither can we.

GRACENOMICS doesn't invalidate a person's legitimate victimization at some point in life; rather it fights a person's impulse to remain a victim—paying for life's traumas again and again throughout life.

Here's what I mean: Experts claim it is possible for a traumatic event to strike us over and over again throughout the course of our lives. Meaning the tragedy impacts us once in the moment when the failure, abuse, or violation took place, and again each time we stew on it, analyze it or talk about it with others.

Giving so much air time to our worst moments can actually impede the healing process.

In Karen Salmansohn's book *The Bounce Back*, for example, she shares from a study performed by famed ethologist Boris Cyrulnik.

In Cyrulnik's study of women whom had experienced sexual trauma he found that when friends expressed too much pity or horror about the woman's experience, this actually escalated the pain and kept the women in "victim mode."

Instead, he found that it was NOT compassion that inspired them to recover but rather being told that they were "strong."

Power words of strength, tenacity, and toughness used in conversation pushed women to believe it was possible for them to buck up and go on.

It is tempting to carve out our identity as victims and recruit a team of supporters to affirm our status.

But if we were honest with ourselves we would see the ongoing injustice and oppression doesn't lie within the event, but in the belief that we are powerless to move on.

It may be time for some of us to plot our escape from Victimville and head on down to Gracetown.

GRACE WANTS TO *heal* YOUR BROKEN HEART

CAN YOU FIND IT?

The second principle of GRACENOMICS FOR YOU is:

FIND THE AWESOME!

Let me give you an example of what I mean:

I read a story about a shoe factory who sends two marketing scouts to a region of Africa to study the prospects for expanding their business. One sends back a telegram saying,

"Situation hopeless. Stop. No one wears shoes."

The other writes back triumphantly,

"Glorious business opportunity. Stop. They have no shoes."

The lesson here? Find the awesome and adjust your perspective.

As Anthony deMello, a Jesuit priest, said it, "No person on earth has the power to make you unhappy."

Rather, deMello insists, it is YOU and YOU ALONE who gives others the power to affect your perspective. You are the one who declares you need specific things—a pay raise, a cordial co-worker, a more ethical boss, a more affectionate spouse, a more loyal friend, or even a smaller butt—to be happy.

Now you may think of yourself as a natural pessimist and cynic.

Maybe you have always been a glass-half-empty kind of person and the Eeyore gene runs in the family. Interestingly enough, scientists behind the U.K.'s "The Happiness Project" have found that while our genetics may influence our perspective, only about 50% of our disposition—our optimism (happiness) or pessimism—is determined by our gene pool.

That makes me wonder, "What if we made a point in life to take control of the other 50%?" Author Neil Pasricha has done just that. He built a successful publishing career on this simple act of finding the awesome.

Pasricha, who considers himself a no-name 30-something, started a blog called *1,000 Awesome Things.* His simple objective? He wanted to find at least one awesome thing about life every day and then post it on his blog.

Moments Neil has found happiness in include:

- When that social event you REALLY didn't want to go to gets cancelled.

- When your guests do the dishes even after you told them not to.

- Biting the last piece of Popsicle without losing any.

- Starting the lawnmower on the first pull.

- When your shoes are tight enough to stay on your foot, but loose enough to slide on and off without untying them.

You say that isn't necessarily profound, but I say it is, because I'd wager that in choosing to filter the world for happiness, Pasricha helped himself become more happy.

I bet he started noticing more happy things.

That the world started seeming more and more dotted by goodness.

The profoundness of this principle hinges on which thing you choose to look for.

Those who practice GRACENOMICS intentionally set out to "find the awesome"—however big or small—in life. Having proper perspective is critical to unleashing second chance living.

DOGGONE IT, PEOPLE LIKE ME

Am I saying pretend the bad doesn't exist? Falsely build up your life with illusions of good?

Not at all.

That is self-esteem. What I'm pushing is self-acceptance.

Here's the difference.

Self-esteem is the trademark of *Saturday Night Live* character self help guru Stuart Smalley played by Al Franken. You might remember the sketches.

Stuart would open a talk show with "Daily Affirmations" like "I deserve good things, I am entitled to my share of happiness. I refuse to beat myself up. I am an attractive person. I am fun to be with." The character was so popular it spawned the novel *I'm Good Enough, I'm Smart Enough, and Doggone It, People Like Me!*

Self-esteem celebrates only the good—or "esteemable"—in us.

Self-acceptance, on the other hand, doesn't just accept the admirable things; it embraces all aspects of ourselves—both positive and negative.

Philosopher Carl Jung developed ideas along these lines. He insisted that everyone—no matter how great—carries a shadow. And he warned, when you choose to ignore the shadow, or to pretend it's not even there, it doesn't fix the bad in you, it just lowers your awareness. This, in turn, makes you susceptible to even greater failures; it leads you to even darker places.

So the third principle in GRACENOMICS FOR YOU requires us to accept our dark and light and:

MAKE FRIENDS WITH OUR SHADOW.

Along these lines, let's try an experiment.

Let's give ourselves permission to fall short. Even if we lose reputation or support because of our failings.

Let's go out of our way to be a little kinder, a little more encouraging, a little more gracious to the losers inside of us.

Anders Ericsson, professor of Psychology at Florida State University, studied great performers. What he found was NOT that great performers didn't fail. They DID screw up. But WHEN they failed, Ericsson found they were better at recovering, making adjustments and learning from their mistakes.

So right now, do yourself a favor. Reach down into your soul and let your failure off the hook.

Have the common sense to approach life the same way you'd approach fishing. Catch and release what's not useful.

Once you accept your failures, you may come to see them less like disasters and more like the driving force behind future successes.

FAIL WASTING AND CHARCOAL MAKING

Mark Horvath founded an organization called *Invisible People* (www.InvisiblePeople.tv). His non-profit organization smashes stereotypes about the plight of America's homeless. He does this by videotaping their stories and using social media to expose the pain, hardship and hopelessness that millions of people face each day.

But what I especially love about Mark is not only his passion to help people, but the fact that Mark was once homeless himself.

Mark could have been ashamed or hid his past. He could have just given up and quit while he was living on the streets. But he

TO UNDERSTAND
THE ENEMY
BOTH WITHIN US AND
OUTSIDE OF US IS AN
IMPORTANT PART
OF FORGIVENESS

- JEAN VANIER

didn't waste this pain or hardship. Instead he leveraged it for others and is now a vocal advocate for the homeless community.

We tend to think of life's lows and valleys as negatives. Garbage. Trash. Junk.

But what if we practiced second chance living and saw the busted up scraps of our life as opportunities just like Mark did?

GRACENOMICS FOR YOU is driven by this final truth:

YOUR FAIL IS NOT WASTE.

As Jason Fried and David Hansson pointed out in their book *Rework*, even waste has value.

The lumber industry has this down. They use sawdust, chips and shredded wood to make fireplace logs, concrete, mulch and particleboard.

Anheuser-Busch turns the beech wood chips it uses to make lager into playground mulch.

Henry Ford figured out how to use the wood scraps from making the Model T and turn it into a successful charcoal business.

What if we were this inventive when it came to hardship? What if we didn't waste our pain, our loss and the learnings from our mistakes?

What useful things might come from our valleys?

Accepting our down side or making the most of our failures doesn't mean we arrogantly dismiss the pain or disappointment we caused others. It also doesn't give us permission to ignore our valleys and not learn from them.

TAKE THE LONG VIEW

Adopting GRACENOMICS IN YOU will take some time.

You will get frustrated as you repeat unhealthy patterns. Your interior world will at times be overrun by the negative insurgency in your mind that reminds you of your past. But don't give up!

Don't abandon grace.

As Anne Morrow Lindbergh, wife of Charles Lindbergh, so aptly stated, "Only when a tree has fallen can you take a measure of it. It is the same with a man."

Don't make the mistake of measuring the value and contribution of your life too soon.

You are not done. You're just getting started. So start dreaming. Practice self-acceptance and get on with it.

The world is waiting for you.

ACTION & INSIGHT

In Episode 11 of the TV show Glee, Quinn, the head-cheerleader-turned-expecting-Mom says, "What I need right now, even more than looser pants, is acceptance."

Too often we are happy to work on someone's problem. We feel good when we can fix things. A lot of us are really skilled at providing "looser pants."

But today give something different. Give acceptance.

Honestly, it's what most of us are really wanting anyways.

NOTES. YOUR THOUGHTS. PERSONAL APPLICATION.

GRACENOMICS FOR OTHERS

THE FORGIVENESS INSTINCT

INVISIBLE PRICETAGS

DON'T TRUST YOUR BLINK BRAIN

GRACE FOR GRACE KILLERS

ADOPT THE POV OF THE OFFENDER

PEOPLE ARE NOT EVIL, THEY ARE WEAK

GRACENOMICS CAN REPAIR THE WORLD

DO THE MATH

PICKAXES & NIBBLED BY DUCKS

When Census worker Sherri Chesney approached a woman working in her garden, she politely introduced herself and showed her Bureau badge. The woman's reaction? "I don't need the blankety-blank government snooping in my business"—a declaration she punctuated by a metal patio table thrown at Chesney.

Shocking? Yes. But it isn't even a singular occurrence.

According to Carol Morello of the *Washington Post*, Census takers have been "shot at with pellet guns and hit by baseball bats. They have been confronted with pickaxes, crossbows and hammers. They've had lawn mowers pushed menacingly toward them and patio tables thrown their way. They have been nibbled by ducks, bitten by pit bulls and chased by packs of snarling dogs."

And it's getting worse, not better.

In 2010, the Census Bureau reported 379 assaults on census workers, almost double the 181 recorded assaults made during the 2000 census.

Citizens' backlash against the census captures a glimpse of the rising hostility emerging in our relationships.

Never before has GRACENOMICS FOR OTHERS been so needed. The census assaults didn't shock me though because I often get a front row seat to observe hostility.

But in many cases, a spot close to the action isn't something to brag about.

As I counsel others, it's often like I have ring-side seats at a MMA match.

I hear every crack and thud of fist meeting flesh and occasionally I have to duck the blood and sweat flying my direction. Some people get off on that. I don't.

The stuff I've seen as people bash out their conflicts is equally capable of making onlookers cringe:

- Best friends rattling off tedious laundry lists of gripes and "hurts" they've been collecting against each other.

- Leaders delivering torturous speeches shifting blame to scapegoat employees.

- Couples ripping on each others inadequacies and lack of understanding.

Any one of these situations could be radically changed—and sometimes were changed—by just a little bit of grace.

That is, if grace was in more plentiful supply.

MONKEY TIME AND THE FORGIVENESS INSTINCT

The thirst for revenge is natural. Instinctive.

Hating on freeloaders, Wall Street types, and people who hurt us is…human.

Payback is in our DNA.

David McCullough, professor of Psychology at the University of Miami and author of the book *Beyond Revenge*, points out that western therapy often sees revenge as a disease. But actually, according to McCullough, revenge is a biological impulse that is part of a creature's innate, hard-wired ability to fight for survival.

Take the Macaque monkey. If a Macaque is harmed by a stronger, more powerful Macaque, even though the victim cannot exact their revenge directly on his stronger offender, he will go out and find the relative of the higher Macaque and harm him instead.

Revenge is natural stuff, although—be warned—McCullough found it can lead to some very ugly behaviors in the long run.

But there is good news. The tendency to forgive is in our DNA too. "The forgiveness instinct is every bit as wired in as the revenge instinct," McCullough said. "It seems that our minds work very hard to get away from resentment, if we can."

And here is the best news of all. McCullough does not believe forgiveness is this enormous, impossible thing for humans to

EVERYONE FORGIVES ME, EXCEPT ME.

practice. Instead, he believes forgiveness is a built-in instinct seen in humans' unique ability to cooperate with others.

McCullough maintains we already forgive in small, routine ways every day. We just need to feed and develop this instinct that is already at work.

INVISIBLE PRICETAGS

Another reality of the human species is that we love to judge, label and assess value.

Recently *Newsweek* did a feature story called *The Beauty Advantage.* In it, reporter Jessica Barnett wrote, "Economists have long recognized what's been dubbed the 'beauty premium'—the idea that pretty people, whatever their aspirations, tend to do better in, well, almost everything."

Handsome men, for example, earn an average of 5% more than their less-attractive counterparts while good-looking women rake in an extra 4%.

They also found that "pretty people get more attention from teachers, bosses, and mentors; even babies stare longer at good-looking faces." Can you believe even babies are in on it?

For some of you this is good news. For the rest of us it is pretty depressing, huh? But before all of us beauty-challenged folks get too huffy-puffy, we must first consider whether we participate in this system too.

I know I do.

Sometimes I act as though it is somehow my job to determine people's worth.

Good looks, lots of cash, a likable personality and the potential to help me in life? I whip out my pricing gun and tag them with a high value.

Run into someone who is a little on the f-ugly side, has low skills and has the potential to damage my reputation with their sordid past?

Bzzt! My pricing gun assigns them a low value that sends them to the clearance rack.

I'm guessing we all get pulled into this sort of pricing game, maybe without realizing what it subtracts from the quality of our lives and relationships.

How many times do we let a misguided fashion sense or blemished complexion cause us to pass over someone who could've genuinely contributed to our development?

How many times have we failed to enjoy the moment we were in because we were so stuck to our judge's clipboard?

The sooner we recognize human life is important— PERIOD—the sooner our lives start to feel more humane.

The worst part is, it's not just strangers that we assault with our pricing guns. Often it's the people we love the most that we treat most harshly.

When it comes to this, I stand among the guilty. I have an incredible wife and two kids who I genuinely cherish, so it stuns me (in retrospect) how I can somehow be so impatient and intolerant toward them.

It makes no sense.

And if you think we're bad to the people we love, think about the people we used to love.

Take our ex-spouses for example. Isn't it amazing how we can come to thrash on a person who we...

- once thought was the funniest, hottest human being on the planet?

- loved enough to make us rent tuxedos, dress up our friends in silly bridesmaid dresses, and drop thousands of dollars on wedding cake and finger sandwiches?

- got naked with and made babies with (or at least enjoy the attempts)?

But now, all of the sudden, these once fabulous, glamorous, intelligent people are the epitome of evil.

I'm not buying it. Our exes can't ALL be mentally deranged monsters.

The more likely scenario is that we let the grace get sucked out of our families and marriages. And it all went downhill from there. Instead of unleashing second chance living we sent it packing.

DON'T TRUST
YOUR BLINK BRAIN

You know what else sucks the grace out of life? Our obsession with speed.

In his best-selling book, *Blink: The Power of Thinking Without Thinking*, Author Malcolm Gladwell encourages readers to use a technique called "thin slicing" to quickly gauge what is important based on gut instinct.

Thin slicing may come in handy in some scenarios, but I'm not convinced it's a good philosophy for approaching people.

Our first impressions are often bigoted and prejudiced. And that squishy little sponge in our cranium can be easily tricked into drawing the wrong conclusions.

Take the first time I met my wife. I totally "thin sliced" her. She walked into an event I was at accompanied by a well-known Don Juan type. I was instantly convinced she was a "blonde floozy" with subpar morals. 5 years later I married her. This year we celebrated our 15th anniversary together.

My "blink" was dead wrong.

Or consider the time I first met Jud Wilhite at a retreat in Palm Springs. I dismissed him as a schmoozing-salesman-consultant type who was too upbeat for my taste. My blink brain whispered in my ears, "Don't trust this dude! He is bad news."

Dead wrong again!

Jud is now my best friend and my closest confidant. Together we founded *People of the Second Chance*.

Sadly, our rushed life has facilitated simplistic opinions, conclusions, and judgments about issues that are ANYTHING but simple.

People. Religion. Values. Sexuality. Race. Marriage. Immigration. Just to name a few.

So do your relationships a favor and slow down.

Do your long-term research.

Respect complexities.

It is key to effective grace giving.

42 OUNCES OF HATER-ADE

So grace for strangers, our families, ex-spouses, opponents and prisoners. We've pretty much covered it, right? Not quite yet.

See, once you adopt grace, the hardest people to show grace to are…the grace killers. The people who ignorantly, perhaps overtly tout their lack of grace.

Think picketers who show up at the funerals of servicemen to protest the United States' engagement in Iraq. Or protestors who wave "God Hates Fags" signs at Gay Pride parades.

On his blog, my friend Pete Wilson noted the ungracious can be the hardest people to treat with grace.

"Grace to prodigals? Yep. Grace to screw ups? No problem.

Grace to self-righteous, pride filled, judgmental types? Ummmmmm, not so quick."

I've got to admit this is a tricky one for me too. I have no patience with people who spew hate and disrespect others.

So when I come across grace killers I feel justified chugging down my own 42-ouncer of hater-ade and giving them a bruise or two to help them re-evaluate.

But GRACENOMICS FOR OTHERS says otherwise.

If we truly want to unleash second chance living we have to show GRACE TO THE GRACE KILLERS.

Why, you ask? Because if you don't extend grace to the grace killers....well....you are one of them.

RELATIONSHIPS

REASON WHY
PEOPLE DON'T
LIKE YOU

JUDGMENTAL

TALENTED
GOOD LOOKING
SMART
SUCCESSFUL

MONSTER MAKEOVERS

So maybe these grace killers need a makeover?

I live in LA, the plastic surgery Mecca of the world. We suck it, pluck it, and plump it like no other. But no matter where you live, Americans tend to be fascinated by extreme makeovers.

GRACENOMICS FOR OTHERS should compel us to give these makeovers—not just to those we naturally empathize with, but to the so-called monsters in our lives.

Here are two steps to start turning a monster back into a human.

STEP 1: OFFER THE PERSON THE SAME HUMANITY YOU USE TO FILTER YOUR OWN LIFE.

If you let yourself get away with a few snarky comments sometimes and chalk it up to a bad day, consider your offender might also be operating out of a similarly frustrating or painful situation. When we acknowledge others' humanness, and as follows their propensity to make mistakes, we are less likely to nurture hate or revenge.

STEP 2: ADOPT THE POINT OF VIEW OF THE OFFENDER.

What would make them see the situation the way they do? Are they afraid of an outcome that will harm them? Are they overly invested and can't afford to lose? Are they emotionally depleted by some other life circumstance? Aim to develop the skill of entertaining how others might look at the situation. The results will be powerful and life altering.

**IF YOU JUDGE PEOPLE,
YOU HAVE NO TIME TO
LOVE THEM.**

-MOTHER TERESA

BALD HEADED MR. EVIL

In the film *Austin Powers*, a United Nations representative makes a major faux pas by referring to Mike Myers' bald headed bad guy as "Mr. Evil." The character responds with disgusted offense, "It's Dr. Evil. I didn't spend six years in Evil Medical School to be called 'Mister,' thank you very much."

Though Dr. Evils do exist in the world, most of our lives are not spent battling bald headed bad guys who went to Evil Medical School.

Instead, we're interacting with Joe who obnoxiously sucks up to the boss and steals our pens. Or Jessie who bailed on our dinner date for the third time…with a last minute text message. Or Kathleen, the manager who constantly talks down to us and makes us feel small.

But I'd like to ask you to entertain a possibility: Maybe it's not that people are evil. Maybe it's that they are weak. Most people don't wake up thinking…*my goal is to inflict unhappiness on as many people as possible.* Most combative adults didn't spend their childhoods dreaming they'd one day become unfeeling social monsters.

Rather, people choose meanness out of impaired vision and skewed understanding. Or as writer and philosopher Mary Wollstonecraft puts it, "No man chooses evil because it is evil; he only mistakes it for happiness."

GRACENOMICS FOR OTHERS involves adopting this perspective:

PEOPLE ARE NOT EVIL, THEY ARE WEAK.

BREATH OF LIFE

Some people seem to be tapping the best parts of their instincts already. Even in a vulture culture they choose to resuscitate the injured rather than feeding on them.

Like what happened when Roncalli, an impressive junior varsity softball team that hadn't lost a single game in two and a half years, was pitted against Marshall—a team playing their first high school game in the school's history.

The game started off with Marshall pitchers walking nine Roncalli batters. The crowd expected a blowout; a game called a "mercy" by the fifth inning.

But Roncalli delivered a different kind of mercy.

Seeing the Marshall girls' enormous disadvantage, Roncalli offered to forfeit and take their first defeat in two and a half years. Instead of thrashing Marshall, they proceeded to spend two hours helping Marshall get better.

As it turned out, Marshall was an under-equipped middle school expanding to include sixth through twelfth grade. The team didn't even have helmets, sliding pads or cleats. Not to mention none of their players or their coach had ever played softball before.

The first lessons were things like, "This is called a batting stance." Soon, the Marshall players were making progress and high-fiving their newfound mentors from Roncalli in celebration.

But the story doesn't end there.

Marshall's coach, a guy named Traylor, started an equipment drive—collecting used athletic equipment for the school and raising $2,500 for the Marshall program. He also found the Marshall coach a mentor in a nearby retiree.

But wait, there's more.

When word got out about what was going on, Reebok found the team free time in a batting cage and the Cincinnati Reds donated infield dirt.

Marshall never won a game all season, but the players and parents got so caught up in the magic of grace, they asked to extend their season into AAU summer softball as well.

Coach Traylor's actions demonstrated three core ideas of GRACENOMICS FOR OTHERS.

1. GRACE IS FREE
Coach Traylor gave and asked nothing in return. He expected nothing from the Marshall players, coaches or fans. This wasn't a career move or an attempt to make headlines. In a world where our relationships are often loaded up with hidden agendas, GRACENOMICS attaches no strings.

2. GRACE IGNORES CATEGORIES
Coach Traylor did not look at the Marshall players as his opponents. The logo on their hats and jerseys was of no significance. Traylor simply saw individuals who needed grace. Just as a lamp gives its light to all, GRACENOMICS gives itself away without discrimination.

3. GRACE IS NOT FORCED UPON ANYONE

A key to the beauty of this story is that Coach Traylor had enough sense to offer to forfeit, not demand it. He let the Marshall coaches and players decide if this GRACENOMICS transaction was going to happen. He did not force this moment of grace upon them.

WORKING FOR AND AGAINST GRACE

One cool part of Coach Traylor's story is that he got a bunch of people engaged in giving grace together. But that isn't always the cultural norm.

When groups don't know any grace based processes for handling difficulty, they may go the opposite direction as Traylor and decide to "get theirs" by any means necessary.

This is true in the school where my friend Sarah works, which is located in a city best known for housing the state prison.

Last year, when a runaway gunman shot one of Sarah's students in the head, the students all claimed to know the identity of the shooter. However, none of them mentioned this to the police.

When Sarah asked why, the students insisted the justice system was broken. They feared that police would prosecute any witnesses as accessories to the crime.

After all, many had family members who claimed they were wrongfully sentenced for crimes they didn't commit.

Instead, Sarah's students told her, "The streets will handle the streets." Translation? The shooter would be "taken care of"... possibly by yet another shooter.

And once again, the community of witnesses would disappear during the police investigation.

Later that year, another student—the brother of the first victim—was shot in an independent incident. Both students miraculously survived.

But the ongoing violence got people in Sarah's community thinking about solutions.

Even the legal system started taking creative approaches to justice.

Unrelated to these shootings, the courts announced they would offer a systemic kind of grace by allowing residents who had unpaid fines, missing court dates or outstanding arrest warrants to turn themselves in and avoid handcuffs.

Instead of being locked up, these residents were invited to see a judge and counselor who would help them set up a manageable plan to pay fines or take care of other obligations to the court.

This amnesty program was designed, a court officer reported, to give people a fresh start.

Can you imagine how the world would change if groups worked for grace instead of against it?

DO THE MATH

So let's get practical here. Every week my wife gives me $40 to cover my Starbucks Grande Mochas, Chick-Fil-A lunches, and Target hair gel.

My goal is to make this last the full seven days. If I blow all my cash at the beginning of the week binging on too many chicken nuggets and cole slaw, I'm stuck inviting myself to business lunches so I can score a free meal.

So imagine with me now, what would happen if we took this simple idea and applied it to grace?

What if we put ourselves on a GRACENOMICS allowance—40 GRACENOMICS bucks is all we get each week.

Here is how it works:

Lose your temper on the freeway and flip someone the bird? Hand over four bucks.

Let your mind dwell on how you hate your boss? Give back three bucks.

Snicker at the fat lady in the grocery store spilling out of her polyester pants? Five bucks.

You get the idea.

It'd be easy to burn through those grace bucks and have almost nothing—except for emotional ugliness—to show for it.

But what if I said you could invest that same currency in grace and double your original investment?

I think that is how grace works.

Actions fueled by grace not only stir immediate goodness, but they compound good like interest.

Judgment or revenge results in a net loss but giving second chances produces a net gain.

Want to build a healthy life portfolio and earn some life-altering returns on your investment?

Sink your money into a few shares of GRACENOMICS for others.

Practicing GRACENOMICS FOR OTHERS is a great place to start when embracing your new second chance life.

If we truly want to liberate love and overthrow judgment, a good place to start is in our relationships.

NOTES. YOUR THOUGHTS. PERSONAL APPLICATION.

ACTION & INSIGHT

Who is the person who you have come to believe you can never, ever forgive? Think of that person now. You know who I'm talking about right?

What is his/her name? Say it out loud. Or write it down...now. And then let today be the day you forgive. And let it go.

This is just for you. Not for them.

For when you forgive you will finally be free.

NOTES. YOUR THOUGHTS. PERSONAL APPLICATION.

GRACENOMICS AT WORK

GRACE IS THE NEW BLACK

PRACTICE THE ART OF GENEROUS LISTENING

TRANSPARENT MISTAKES

CELEBRATE ALL VALUE CREATION

DON'T BE SO DANG SERIOUS

DON'T DISS YOUR DISASTERS

PEOPLE MATTER

GRACE IS THE NEW BLACK

It sorta makes sense, intuitively, that showing more grace could positively impact our personal lives and relationships.

But it may be more surprising to find that GRACENOMICS has serious pay off in the business world as well. And by payoff, I don't just mean grace generates warm and fuzzy feelings at the company Christmas party. I mean grace pays off in the well being of employees and the bottom line.

Take, for instance, the time our design firm, PlainJoe Studios, brought in consultants to help analyze our company history and identify factors that contributed to our success.

We were hoping to snag a few insights from the consulting team. Maybe walk away understanding our "personality" a bit better. What we got though was an unexpected lesson in GRACENOMICS.

The consultants started investigating why clients chose PlainJoe Studios in the first place and, more importantly, why they stayed with us.

After extensive surveying of our clients they found that though they rated our design, creativity and services at a very high level, the reason clients stayed was because they felt loved and valued.

Customers reported that we not only cared deeply about the success of their organization, but that we also cared about them as individuals. They trusted that we had their best interest at heart. We worked hard to understand their perspective when problems arose on a project and we talked transparently about how we could do better the next time.

These results underlined something for me. That GRACENOMICS has implications for endless areas of our lives. It can make our work world, and so much more beyond, a better place to be.

Look at how the companies below have adopted grace and empathy for others as a corporate value:

Best Buy donates about 1% of its pre-tax profit to charities, especially those impacting children.

Gap contributes half of its profit from the sale of its (Product) Red merchandise to the Global Fund, which combats HIV/AIDS in Africa.

Kohl's raises more than $102 million per year using its Cares for Kids program, which puts 100% of its profits from stuffed animals and books toward children's health and education.

Even the organization I lead, People of the Second Chance, is in on the action too. We turned a 1970 Cadillac De Ville into a "museum on wheels" to help bring awareness and raise $50,000 for the mobile homeless community. The mobile homeless are people forced to live in their vehicles due to hard financial times. You can find out more at www.POTSC.com.

When it comes to worthy causes, almost everyone is helping. And that being the case, no one wants to be caught being the only business who isn't.

Why are companies racing to get in on the goodness? We hope attitudes of goodwill are prevailing. But also, remember what I said earlier. Grace is spurring more than just a little positive PR. It can also energize a company's bottom line.

Research from Cone Communications showed that shampoo sold to benefit a charitable cause saw a 74 percent sales increase over the same brand without a cause.

In addition, Dover Management found companies who committed operating earnings to charitable giving outperformed the Standard & Poor's 500 index by 3.5 percentage points over five years.

Grace is the new black!

The careful critics among you might be protesting, but wait a minute, is giving to a good cause really grace??

Isn't grace more about forgiving people or accepting them as they are?

Sure. It's those things, but grace isn't a small-scale idea limited by a dictionary definition. It's a concept with muscles and teeth that shows strength outside of its conventional applications, which is exactly why it belongs in a competitive business world.

Here's what I mean: Think of a person you would consider gracious. What makes that person gracious in your eyes? Is it just that they go around forgiving people left and right? Or is "grace" a broader umbrella term that covers a whole family of behaviors—everything from being tactful to responding responsibly to conflict?

WE CAN NOT CHANGE
WHAT WE DO NOT
NOTICE.

-TONY SCHWARTZ

When we think of Big-G Grace as something that goes well beyond just forgiveness, we start to see endless applications for grace in the workplace.

One of them, for example, might be found in the practice of listening well.

GENEROUS LISTENING

Unfortunately the skill of effective listening sometimes gets lost in a tweet-happy world obsessed with announcing every mundane teeth-brushing-left-turn-signaling-searching-for-the-remote-control move.

We pride ourselves on our proclamations, not on being good listeners.

Researcher Linda Stone calls our poor listening habits "Continuous Partial Attention." In short, we half-heartedly listen to the person speaking to us so we scan the periphery for more important things going on.

We communicate to people that they aren't valuable enough to deserve our undivided attention.

Listening becomes defined as "what you pretend to do while waiting for the other person to shut up so you can talk again." In short, we don't really give a damn. But giving a damn is part of being that gracious person, don't you think?

GRACENOMICS says wherever you are, be fully there.

On the other hand, those who give their full attention to others are winning big.

Case in point? Zappos.com.

Tony Hsieh started Zappos in 1999 as an online shoe store. In 2008, Zappos recorded $1 billion in gross sales, which was a 20 percent increase over the year before.

What is Zappos getting right? One thing they're doing well is listening.

Get this. The Zappos call center bucks the standard for responding to customer calls. They don't use scripts. They don't try to limit time per call. And they don't badger the customer with additional sales pitches for products or services unrelated to the reason for the call.

Hsieh, in fact, proudly boasts that the longest call in Zappos history was FOUR hours!! He compassionately admits that, "some people are just lonely." Listening to them isn't about just solving a client issue, it's about showing radical devotion to the customer.

Another example of Zappos practicing generous listening came when Zaz Lamarr experienced the death of her mother.

In the middle of trying to get a pair of shoes returned, Lamarr mentioned that her mother had just passed away.

The next day a florist delivered white lilies and carnations to her door. She opened the card to discover that the flowers had

"HOW DOES ONE BECOME

A BUTTERFLY?" SHE

ASKED. "YOU MUST

WANT TO FLY SO MUCH

THAT YOU ARE WILLING

TO GIVE UP BEING

A CATERPILLAR."

- ANONYMOUS

been sent by Zappos. In writing about it, Lamarr said, "I burst into tears…and if that isn't one of the nicest things I've ever had happen to me, I don't know what is."

TRANSPARENT MISTAKES

Few would question the pure genius of billionaire Warren Buffet and his ability to make money. After all, between 1964 to 2007, Buffet lead Berkshire Hathaway to an overall gain of 400,863 percent.

In Joseph Hallinan's brilliant book, *Why We Make Mistakes*, he describes the biggest mistake Buffett ever made in business. Buffet bought the Dexter Shoe Company for $433 million in 1993 declaring it was "one of the best managed companies I have seen in my business lifetime." But in only a few years the purchase tanked and Dexter Shoe Company went out of business.

Whoops.

But that was just the beginning of Buffet's problems. He had paid for the shoe company with 25,203 shares of Class A Berkshire Hathaway stock. So instead of paying $433 million for the failed company he actually ended up paying $3.5 billion.

Double whammy.

So obviously this decision alone isn't what earns Buffett a place in the GRACENOMICS hall of fame.

Rather, it was what he did next.

Buffet fully owned his disastrous decision, explaining to shareholders, "I gave away 1.6% of a wonderful business— one now valued at $220 billion—to buy a worthless business."

This demonstrates another important of GRACENOMICS AT WORK principle:

TRANSPARENT LEADERSHIP.

In a 2007 letter Buffet even warned his shareholders, "I'll make more mistakes in the future...you can bet on that." He didn't conceal his mistakes, he revealed them.

Did Warren Buffet's future as an investor go under after that? Nope. In choosing to be honest, Warren gave his funders an unusual gift: the opportunity to show him grace.

Or try another example.

In Charlene Li's book *Open Leadership*, she tells the story of Sheryl Sandberg, a 37-year-old vice president at Google who made a million dollar mistake. When Sandberg realized the size of her mistake she immediately went to co-founder Larry Page and informed him of this costly error.

Sandberg profusely apologized to Page and explained how she was moving too fast, made a really bad decision and cost the company some serious cash.

I don't know Sandberg personally, but I'm guessing she was shaking in her heels. Most of us would probably walk into that situation with the contents of our desks already packed and in hand.

Even at a billion dollar company like Google, a million bucks is still a million bucks.

But Page was one of those Big G-gracious people. In an incredible move, he accepted her apology. And, to make the story even more startling, he stopped her on the way out of the office to say, "I'm so glad you made this mistake. Because I want to run a company where we are moving too quickly and doing too much—not being too cautious and doing too little. If we don't have any of these mistakes, we're just not taking enough risk."

Li goes on to tell of her conversation with Chris DiBona, the open source and public sector manager at Google, who explained, "Google does more than tolerate failure grudgingly— it actively creates a support system for people so that they feel comfortable failing."

Google has mastered the idea of creating a safe environment where employees can take risks, try new things and feel safe. They're shielding their employees under the affirming umbrella of grace. They practice GRACENOMICS and have a second chance culture.

So how do we develop this same culture of GRACENOMICS that can balance failure and grace?

1. CELEBRATE ALL VALUE CREATION
Our definition of value has been hijacked by speed of growth, prominence and attention. But it is critical for all of us to understand that the true worth of an idea isn't determined by whether our efforts are showcased in the New York Times or

whether we have 500,000 Facebook Fans.

Value creation happens when someone is impacted for the good, lives are changed, people are transformed and the organization's mission moves forward.

Too often we overlook the killer project happening right in front of us because it's just not sexy. In short, grace isn't always sexy. But, on the flip side, you don't regret grace the next morning.

2. DON'T BE SO DANG SERIOUS
Ready to hear something outlandish?

At Zappos, managers are now required to spend 10 to 20 percent of their time goofing off with the people they manage. Yes, you read that right. Goofing off and having fun. Sorry people, it's company policy. You'll have to comply.

I know, I know. A lot of our work is important. The stakes are high. But holy cow do we need a good dose of perspective sometimes. I wonder how much more grace would flow if companies replaced their break room coffee with some economy sized bottles of chill pills.

3. DON'T DISS YOUR DISASTERS
As you read this next section, please pull out your Newton and take notes.

My what?

Your Newton. Haven't heard of it? Exactly.

Before Apple sold 2 million iPads in just 2 months, they failed at launching a gadget known as the Newton. The Newton was the first tablet platform Apple developed that the public rejected. Though the device never really caught on, it certainly can be seen as a pre-cursor to the smashing success of the iPad and a legitimate part of the iPad's developmental story.

If, in their frustration over the Newton's failure, Apple had buried the failure, abandoned the tablet model and shuffled back to a desktop or laptop niche, they would've missed out on the cultural craze caused by the Ipad.

Too often we want to pretend that failed ventures never happened. We erase them from the history books. But what is even worse is that we make the mistake of pretending our failures have no impact or relevancy on what is working well today.

But what if instead of being dishonest about our disasters, we learned to show them a little respect? What if, as leaders, we spoke openly about struggle, failure and the honesty of our checkered pasts? How much more growth would come out of the truth that surfaced?

With a little grace in the workplace, how many more iPad-level successes would the world have seen?

DON'T MAKE YOUR COMPANY MASCOT THE SCAPEGOAT

What about us? Are we okay with failures that surface across the lifespan of our organizations?

You may know from personal experience that there are no winners in a company game of blame.

When team members see a leader place blame on a scapegoat, or when they see a teammate harshly reprimanded, it sends out a universal message:

Be afraid. Be very afraid.

Here's what I mean.

The boss pretends the company never fails. Never has, never will.

The employees know this is a bunch of bull. Always has been, always will be.

But because they know their boss is fixated with erasing all evidence of the company's failures, the employees trade in the goal of advancing the company for the boss' real goal: covering up mistakes—along with anything that might've been learned from them.

Creativity is choked out.

Innovators are handcuffed.

Dreams die.

Makes you wonder how much money companies have lost because employees buried great ideas in fear of failure, doesn't it?

In order for GRACENOMICS AT WORK to be effective:

ACCOUNTABILITY AND TRUTH MUST RIEGN SURPREME.

Nobody wants to play games or politics. It is a drain on the organization and slows the speed and efficiency of a company.

A popular website asks people to submit how they've been screwed by friends, lovers, and employers. Consider this entry on the site:

Today, my boss fired me because he said I was spending too much time surfing the internet.

When I reminded him that my work computer isn't even networked, he said, "Oh, sorry, you're the one who takes too many smoke breaks."

When I told him that I don't even smoke, he said, 'Just go..."

Funny, huh?

Less funny, I bet, is how many employees would paint their bosses in a similar light.

TO BE UNAWARE OF YOUR
OWN POWER IS ALMOST
AS IRRESPONSIBLE AS
BEING AWARE, & USING
IT IRRESPONSIBLY.

-MARCUS BUCKINGHAM

NOTES. YOUR THOUGHTS. PERSONAL APPLICATION.

GRACENOMICS LEADERSHIP

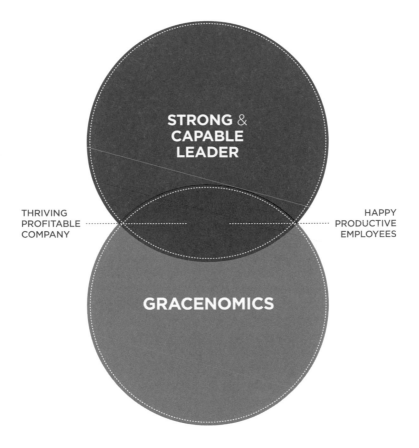

STRONG & CAPABLE LEADER

THRIVING PROFITABLE COMPANY

HAPPY PRODUCTIVE EMPLOYEES

GRACENOMICS

PEOPLE MATTER

Along these lines, I once worked for a non-profit organization that didn't have the guts to fire underperforming employees. Instead of sitting employees down for a direct and honest performance review, the organization unpacked their "feedback" through passive aggressive tactics.

They would:

- turn up the heat.

- try to make the employee feel uncomfortable.

- become hypercritical of the employee's day to day work.

- purposefully assign the employee tasks outside his skill area or job description hoping for them to become frustrated and feel insecure.

- constantly transfer the employee to a new department to keep them unsettled.

But this kind of lack of grace not only smacks of cruelty, but it flies in the face of sound research. Researchers point out that the number one factor influencing employee retention and performance is whether they feel respected and considered a valuable part of the company.

Yet when the research group Towers Perrin did a massive worldwide survey of 90,000 employees, they found that few companies actually convinced employees they cared. Only 38% of employees felt senior management was interested in their well being. Half of those surveyed said they are treated like they don't matter at all and only 1 out of 10 feel they are treated as vital corporate assets.

Ahhh, you may be protesting, but that is how the business world works. It's cutthroat. It's dog eats dog. It's every man for itself. But I'm here to tell you that GRACENOMICS—adopting more grace in even the capitalistic workplace—makes BUSINESS SENSE.

Go ahead. Follow the trail of logic for yourself.

Which organization would you be more likely to work hard for? Someone who judged you ruthlessly? Or someone who gave you room to grow and improve?

Which would you be less likely to steal from? One that treated you with grace? Or one that treated you like you were discardable?

Which one would you brag about to your networks in the community? The one that gave you honest fair feedback or the one that left you cryptic and critical memos?

GRACENOMICS AT WORK well...simply works. And though it may seem to buck the tradition of cutthroat capitalism, organizations are finally waking up to its power. It is no longer just a nice idealistic dream discussed in academic hallways; it is a proven killer move for successful companies.

ACTION & INSIGHT

Are you safe? Or are you savvy? Let's find out. Below, circle the statements that best apply to you.

Safe people blend in.
Savvy people stand out.

Safe people care about looks.
Savvy people embrace the ugly.

Safe people protect what they've got.
Savvy people risk losing it all.

Safe people are content with status quo.
Savvy people want to change the world.

Safe people are liked.
Savvy people are envied.

Safe or savvy? It's your choice.

ACTION & INSIGHT

Are you fearleading or cheerleading your team? Statistics show that only 10 percent of employees feel like they are valued at work. Most feel unconnected and unappreciated.

Write down 3 names of people you need to express your appreciation to.

OK. So you know those 3 names you just wrote down? Call them right now. Or better yet walk over to their deskand tell them in person. (And emailing doesn't count.)

Tell them that you appreciate their hard work. Be a cheerleader. Not a fearleader.

NOTES. YOUR THOUGHTS. PERSONAL APPLICATION.

JOIN THE SCANDAL

YOUR INVITATION

Grace is scarce. You know it and so do I. So the real question is, "What are we going to do about it?"

Only you, the readers, can move grace off the pages of this book and into your homes, communities and organizations.

Leadership guru Bill Hybels says that people will never drift into better behaviors. We have to be called to it and asked to take our actions up a level.

So with all the boldness that I can muster, I want to invite you to give second chance living a shot. I want you to join the thousands of people who have decided to be GRACENOMIC junkies.

Who are these grace dispensers who have unleashed second chance living?

David is a Grammy winning music producer and Tony is a minister in Orange County.

Sarah is a writer who lives in Michigan.

William runs a multimillion-dollar energy company and Kristen loves being a Mom.

Radical-gracers include a Pulitzer Prize winning news reporter and Shawn, who is a Chick-Fil-A owner.

OVERTHROW JUDGMENT. LIBERATE LOVE.

we are people of the second chance.

Steve is a coach and Scott runs a charity that brings clean water to Africa.

We come from all walks of life and all coordinates on the globe.

We have all tasted the bitterness of failure but we all believe in the power of grace.

This is your personal invite to be part of the scandal and promote an economy of grace.

It is time to unleash the transforming power of second chance living.

ACTION & INSIGHT

Unfortunately, the world will not become a place where things are fair.

Your life will still have pain and disappointment.

Friends will still let you down. There will always be victims and perpetrators.

As long as you are breathing, these things will not change.

But your attitudes and beliefs about grace can radically shift. And it is in that beautiful moment, that everything has the possibility to change.

Instead of trying to change things that are unchangeable, why not spend that energy growing yourself?

WE ARE **PEOPLE OF THE SECOND CHANCE**

Scuba Steve
Jose Luis Liano Sr.
Dee Springer
Michael Palmer
Otto Wiskerchen
Timothy M. Jessen
Jason Bedell
Darren and Thilani Grubel
Mike Zito
Sandra Hiebert
Amber Duke
Vicki Hanes
Adriana Féliz
Bonnie Irving
Dan Rodriguez
Chris Huelat
Randy Sherwood
Jarrid Wilson
Shawn and Pamela Hunter
John and Stefanie Cassetto
Josh Sabo
Candace Ryder
David and Christine Lee
Tim Bogus
Jordan & Sammy Plumier
Ross, Amy, Aiden & Eli Middleton
Stephen Whiting
Bruce & Sarah Horstman
Shelley Egeland
Jordan Bickimer
Kevin Twombly

Scott King
Noah Gonzales
Becca Carroll
Suzanne Beaudoin
Kim Cook
Blake Ryan
Katie Hanner
Jamie Doyle
Debbie Howard Powell
Kristen Powell
John Sahid
Kevin Davis
Frances Hooker
David Phillips
Joshua Webb
Sarah Twilley
Phyllis Neriah
Samantha Bean
Bruce Cole
Marilou Schnaderbeck
Erik Willits
Aaron Bell
Peter McGowan
Colleen Bell
Elijah Bell
McVehil Bell
Melanie McGaughey
Deborah Hardy
James Dawson
Melissa Goldsmith
Robert Glenn Smith

Ryan Moede
Arthur Hsu
Bryan Cawley
Nicolás Jurado
J.D. Eddins
Torri Liano
Mike Knott
Maria Stewart
John M. Palmer
Michele McCullough
Dan McCullough
Steven Vidal
Hope Huska & Kevin Huska
Serena Woods
Matt Svajda
Jay Sauser
Dennis Arriaga
Ben Dubow
Jeff Goins
Ashley & Ryan Smith
Taylor Lyall
Karen Globig
Darcy Knight
Jen Burns
Mike Burns
Dave Marrett
Bill (cycleguy) Grandi
Micaela Neira
Charles Craft
Jonathan Jones
Chris Loach
Rachel Tweet
Kenyon Gerbrandt
Kevin Trobaugh
Lisa Barrett
Steve Barrett

Daniel Ferdinand
Jeremy Glaze
Andy Denen
Ethan Plumier
Angela Kimble
Rodney Eason
Neil & Brandi Schori
Andrea Burnett
Kirk Longhofer
Molly McMahan
AJ Martin
Benjamin Zimmerman
Ashley Zimmerman
Alexis Zimmerman
Lisa Muñoz
Matthew & Kelly Nolasco
Trevor & Julie Buehler
Matt and Lori Albee
Brittany Conley
Emily Blesse
Jack J. Foley
Andy and Jackie Rodgers
Tim S. Wright
Nick Tonti
Lyle A. Peluso
Mike Salomonson
Sherry Young
Sam Nelson
Alan Bell
Vitorya Anderson
Valerie Dykes
Kevin Martineau
Marcus Kirtley
David Joshua
Ric Stevens
Bill Hale

Kyle L Reed
Greg Memberto
Judy Booth
Jason Bunch
Mike Goldsworthy
Joshua White
Johnny Wolinski
Jeff Rush
Justin Sytsma
David Trotter
Carol Asher
Dionna Nalls
Carol Parker
Danny and Karen Hammons
Blake Howard
Vicky Taylor
Sarah Newton
Jonathan Sigmon
Sherie Drew
Kurt Libby
Erika Brinks
Josh Brickey
Lauren Schin
Laura Martin
Matt Saffer
Shannon Overpeck
Kris DeFilippis
Deana and Colin Beers
Greg Darley
Robin Cooper
Heather Rose-Chase
Dustin Valencia
Shelley Stenglein
Anthony Fisher
Todd Stephens
Paul Walaszek

Justin Salters
Jeff Spielman
Kevin Friedemann
Becky Kenealy
Joshua McAfee
Deakin Nash
Mohan Karulkar
Danny Bixby
Tim Mason
Angela Braun
Johny Paul
CJ Casciotta
Nolan Bobbitt
Russell Hawkins
Casey Freeman
Evan McElrath
Billy Ritchie
Charis Lykins
David Buckham
Jillian Rose Peluso
Matthew R. Hexter
Lyle Peluso Jr.
Lindsay Guard
Ryan Guard
Jenny Knoblock
Jeffrey Nickowski
Angus and Samantha Nelson
Ross and Taya Black
Aaron and Jennifer Smith
Kyle King
Christy Leake
Jason Leake
Rocco Capra
Whit Stiles
Jason Wert
David Graves

Laura Anne Mackay
Christopher Wiseman
Ryan Reed
David Terrell
Vikki Huisman
Amy Brown
Megan Lane
Kristan Holding
Sam Frederick
Jack Schull
Carrie Stricklin
Mark McGowan
Nicole Wick
Rick Davidson
Richard Jett
Matt Appling
Jordan Chesbrough
Josh Mauldin
Bryan Allain
Renee Johnson

AND OVER **10,000 OTHER GRACE DISPENSERS!**

CONTACT

CONTACT MIKE:
Mike@POTSC.com

SPEAKING AND BOOKING INQUIRIES:
Kristen@POTSC.com

QUESTIONS AND FEEDBACK:
Contact@POTSC.com

WEBSITE:
www.POTSC.com

ABOUT THE AUTHOR

For the past 10 years Mike Foster has been innovating and creating new ways to experience life transformation. He is an author, speaker and consultant who coaches leaders across the country on personal sustainability and life management.

Mike leads "People of the Second Chance" which is an organization that helps individuals and teams survive and thrive after personal or organizational failure. He serves on the executive team of PlainJoe Studios and as an advisor for the Q and Catalyst leadership conferences.

Mike has appeared as a guest on Good Morning America, FoxNews, CNN, The Dave Ramsey Show, and has been featured in the New York Times, LA Times, GQ, and on The Daily Show with Jon Stewart.

Mike lives in Southern California with his wife and 2 young children.

He blogs daily at www.POTSC.com and is @MikeFoster on Twitter.

NEXT STEPS

GRACENOMICS FOR GROUPS
The concepts of GRACENOMICS are best experienced within the community context. Discuss key issues, increase trust and help develop both personal and organizational relationships within your group. We offer tools to facilitate GRACENOMICS for teams, staffs or small groups as well as bulk discounts on the book.

ONLINE
Join the dynamic community of second chancers at www.POTSC.com. In addition to new insights and resources, we also host LIVE online events. You can also connect with us on the following social networks:

Facebook: www.Facebook.com/POTSC
Twitter: @POTSC and @MikeFoster

MOBILE
Download our FREE People of the Second Chance
Iphone app through Itunes to keep up to date with
new blog posts, photos and videos.

SPEAKING
Mike Foster is available to present on the core issues
of GRACENOMICS and how to unleash second
chance living. Through a passionate and relevant
presentation, Mike addresses the key issues of how
to be a grace dispenser in your relationships and
organizations. Filled with practical next steps and
insights, the dynamic message of GRACENOMICS
will inspire and transform. For speaking inquiries
and a list of presentation topics, please email
Kristen@POTSC.com

PEOPLE
OF THE
SECOND
CHANCE

MIKE FOSTER

COMING FALL OF 2011 FROM HARPER ONE PUBLISHING

What happens when your personal life falls apart?

What do you do after you've driven your career off into a ditch?

Where do you start when you've hit rock bottom?

People of the Second Chance is the brand new book from Mike Foster. In this full color hardback book, Mike delivers a practical guide to reinventing failure, leveraging pain for good, and how to risk it all again.

Through red-hot relevant insights and inspiring stories, *People of the Second Chance* will be the playbook for transforming your life.

ACKNOWLEDGEMENTS

Jennifer, Jackson and Taylor Foster for modeling grace every day to your husband and Dad. Love and kisses.

Bill Townsend for your wisdom, encouragement and commitment to the cause of second chances. I'm soooooo lucky to have you as my friend, mentor and advocate.

Steve Graves for leading me through the wilderness and helping me find my way.

Sarah Cunningham for helping craft this book and bringing so much to this project.

Jud Wilhite for being my best friend and helping me lead the grace revolution. This is going to be fun!

Bill and Jean Foster and Larry, Mary Lou, and the entire Michalski family for your love.

Gabe Lyons and Brad Lomenick for always standing in my corner. Big thanks to the Axiom and Catalyst communities.

Thank you to Becca, Noah and Suzanne for working so hard on this book and the super talented PlainJoe team of Richard, Bree, Johnny, Cliff, Scott, Lauren, Kai, Maureen, Kelly, Kirk, Julie, Ed, Michael, Pat, A, Sheri, Joe and Sarah.

Special thanks to Peter McGowan and Blake Ryan for their support and belief in second chances.

Kristen for being the best Executive Assistant in the world and making a hard job look easy.

Tony Wood, Wess Stafford, Carlos Whittaker, Scott Hodge, Tom Rinks, Jon Acuff, Scott Harrison, David Hodges, Anne Jackson, Jeannie Mai, Darren Whitehead, Greg Spencer, Dino Rizzo and Anne Lamott who continually inspire me with how you live your lives.

Chris Ferebee for your friendship and Yates and Yates for paying attention to the details.

Jim, Jordan, Josh and all the POTSC volunteers who have given so much to the cause.

Jeff Brazil and Kevin Small for your wisdom and expertise.

Dave Gibbons and the Newsong Global Alliance, especially those at Newsong Bangkok who made us feel so at home.

Radiohead, Jonsi and Jon Foreman for providing the soundtrack to this book.

Mike, Murph, Kurt and the entire Central Vegas Family for letting me be a part of your community.

Trever Hoehne, Daley Hake and Holly Pollock for sharing your talents.

I'm grateful to Nick and Dave at Prolifik Films and Steve Carr at Flannel for your ability to tell stories.

And to the People of the Second Chance who live out grace daily. You are my heroes.

ORGANIZATIONS WE LOVE

COMPASSION INTERNATIONAL
Helping over 1 million children living in extreme poverty in over
26 countries. Sponsor a child today at www.Compassion.com

CHARITY: WATER
Charity Water is a non-profit bringing clean and safe drinking
water to people in developing nations.

GIFTCARDGIVER.COM
Collecting and distributing gift cards to help
non-profit organizations.

NOT FOR SALE
Not For Sale equips smart activists to fight the global slave
trade and end human trafficking.

THE MENTORING PROJECT
Responding to the American crisis of fatherlessness through
mentoring boys.

TO WRITE LOVE ON HER ARMS
A movement dedicated to finding help for people struggling with
depression, addiction, self-injury and suicide.

HOPE INTERNATIONAL
Implementing sound microfinance and basic business training
that enable clients in poverty.

INVISIBLEPEOPLE.TV
A non-profit organization smashing stereotypes about the plight
of America's homeless.

DESIGNED BY

STRATEGIC IDEATION. INTERACTIVE MEDIA.
ENVIRONMENTAL DESIGN.

WWW.PLAINJOESTUDIOS.COM

ENDNOTES

White Flag Project, "History" www.WhiteFlagMusic.com (2010)

Erik Hayden, "Today's College Students Lacking Empathy" (Miller-McCune, May 31, 2010)

This American Life, "Neighbors" (This American Life, May 11 2001, #184)

A.J. Jacobs, "I Think You're Fat" (Esquire, July 24, 2007)

Andrea Canning/Kelly Hagan, "Worst Sportsmanship? Dirty Soccer Video Goes Viral" (ABC News, November 9, 2009)

Roy Williams, "Accidental Magic: The Wizard's Techniques for Writing Words Worth 1,000 Pictures" (Bard Press)

Karen Salmansohn, "The Bounce Back Book: How to Thrive in the Face of Adversity, Setbacks, and Losses" (Workman Publishing Company)

Neil Pasricha, "The Book of Awesome: Snow Days, Bakery Air, Finding Money in Your Pocket, and Other Simple, Brilliant Things" (Amy Einhorn Books/Putnam)

Daniel Coyle, "The Talent Code: Greatness Isn't Born. It's Grown. Here's How." (Bantam)

Jason Fried and David Hansson, "Rework" (Crown Business)

Carol Morello, "An Unexpected Result For Some Census Takers: The Wrath of Irate Americans" (Washington Post, June 20, 2010)

Michael McCullough, "Beyond Revenge: The Evolution of the Forgiveness Instinct" (Jossey-Bass Publishing)

Jessica Bennett, "The Beauty Advantage" (Newsweek, July 19, 2010)

Malcolm Gladwell, "Blink: The Power of Thinking Without Thinking" (Little, Brown and Company)

Rick Reilly, "For Love of the Game" (ESPN Online, May 2010)

Max Chafkin, "The Zappos Way of Managing" (Inc Magazine, May 2009)

Joseph T. Hallinan, "Why We Make Mistakes: How We Look Without Seeing, Forget Things in Seconds, and Are All Pretty Sure We Are Way Above Average" (Crown Archetype, February 17, 2009)

Charlene Li, "Open Leadership: How Social Technology Can Transform the Way You Lead" (Jossey-Bass)

WE ARE POTSC